SECOND EDITION

English Across the Curriculum

Content-area Vocabulary and Skills

2

Margaret Martin Maggs

National Textbook Company
a division of NTC/CONTEMPORARY PUBLISHING GROUP
Lincolnwood, Illinois USA

ISBN: 0-8442-0290-8

Published by National Textbook Company,
a division of NTC/Contemporary Publishing Group, Inc.,
4255 West Touhy Avenue,
Lincolnwood (Chicago), Illinois 60646-1975 U.S.A.

8 9 0 VP 9 8 7 6 5 4 3

Contents

Alphabetical Order

What do you know about alphabetical order?

There are twenty-six letters in the English alphabet. Every English student should know the alphabet. The letters are:

It is important to know the order of the alphabet. It is often used to organize books and parts of books. It helps you find words in a dictionary, for example. It helps you find which book to use in an encyclopedia of many books.

Sometimes alphabetical order uses only the letters, like this:

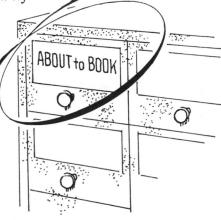

Sometimes, especially in a library, alphabetical order is by the first letter of names or words.

What do you know about alphabetical order?

A   Put the letters in alphabetical order.

EXAMPLE: B, C, A   _____*A, B, C*_____

1. O, N, M   _____   8. V, W, U   _____

2. T, U, S   _____   9. B, D, C   _____

3. D, F, E   _____   10. N, P, O   _____

4. Y, Z, X   _____   11. H, J, I   _____

5. J, L, K   _____   12. X, Y, W   _____

6. P, R, Q   _____   13. F, E, G   _____

7. I, H, G   _____   14. U, V, T   _____

B   Put the words in alphabetical order.

1. job   _____*apple*_____   8. reference   _____

2. can   _____   9. song   _____

3. zebra   _____   10. plant   _____

4. man   _____   11. bank   _____

5. apple   _____   12. look   _____

6. woman   _____   13. television   _____

7. girl   _____   14. ugly   _____

More about Alphabetical Order

What do you know about alphabetical order?

In alphabetical order, sometimes there are two words that begin with the same letter. An example of this is **and** and **apple**. What do you do then? You use the second letter to help you alphabetize (put in alphabetical order). In the word **and** the second letter is <u>N</u>. In the word **apple** the second letter is <u>P</u>. <u>N</u> is before <u>P</u> in the alphabet. The word **and** is before **apple** in alphabetical order.

Here are some more examples:

<u>Science</u>	comes before	<u>Social Studies</u>
<u>little</u>	comes before	<u>love</u>
<u>man</u>	comes before	<u>me</u>

What do you do when the second letter is the same? An example of this is **boy** and **box**. You use the third letter to help you alphabetize. In the word **boy** the third letter is <u>Y</u>. In the word **box** the third letter is <u>X</u>. <u>X</u> is before <u>Y</u> in the alphabet. The word **box** is before **boy** in alphabetical order.

Here are some more examples:

<u>sing</u>	comes before	<u>six</u>
<u>woman</u>	comes before	<u>wood</u>
<u>tree</u>	comes before	<u>try</u>

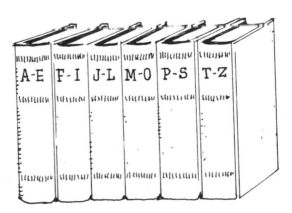

What do you know about alphabetical order?

A Put the words in alphabetical order.

1. eleven, easy   *easy, eleven*   6. love, like   _____

2. dark, dry   _____   7. play, part   _____

3. round, right   _____   8. no, nice   _____

4. sing, song   _____   9. book, bank   _____

5. go, green   _____   10. emergency, excellent   _____

_____

B Put these words in alphabetical order:

1. tame, take   *take, tame*   6. had, have   _____

2. open, opaque   _____   7. love, look   _____

3. name, nail   _____   8. student, stand   _____

4. fan, fat   _____   9. find, fill   _____

5. three, this   _____   10. think, they   _____

C Put these words in alphabetical order:

1. like, lemon, linen   *lemon, like, linen*   6. stop, slow, student   _____

2. chance, cheer, car   _____   7. bill, bank, book   _____

3. vowel, very, veil   _____   8. eat, every, emergency   _____

4. more, mess, moon   _____   _____

5. have, has, hat   _____   9. the, too, thing   _____

10. do, dear, dead   _____

The Library

What words do you know in the library?

Our school has a library. We went there with our teacher.
Words that we used were: <u>alphabetical order</u>, <u>reference</u>,
<u>catalog</u>, <u>card</u>, <u>subject</u>, <u>title</u> and <u>author</u>.

In the library the books are in alphabetical
order. There are many different reference
books we can use.

When we want a book, we look in the
catalog to see where it is.

We can look at the catalog under the
subject.

> RAIN FORESTS
> J/574.52642/ Carey, Helen H.
> CAR   The Rain Forest / Helen H. Carey
>   Milwaukee: Raintree Publishers, 1990.

We can look at the catalog card under
the title. If the title begins with "A,"
"An," or "The," look under the next
word in the title.

> The Rain Forest
> J/574.52642/ Carey, Helen H.
> CAR   The Rain Forest / Helen H. Carey

We can also look at the catalog card under
the author's last name.

> J/574.52642/ Carey, Helen H.
> CAR   The Rain Forest / Helen H. Carey
>   Milwaukee: Raintree Publishers, 1990.

Library

Our teacher took the class to the school library yesterday.
We looked for books to read. We looked in the card
catalog. The cards have the title of the book and the
author's name. The cards are in alphabetical order.

What words do you know in the library?

A Draw a line from the picture to the word.

WORDS

alphabetical order

reference book

card catalog

card

subject

title

author

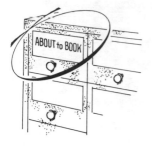

The Rain Forest
J/574.52642/   Carey, Helen H.
CAR   The Rain Forest / Helen H. Carey.
               Milwaukee: Raintree Publishers, 1990.
               32 p.:   col. ill.;   25 cm.

Helen H. Carey

The Rain Forest

B Write the letter you use in the card catalog for a book:

1. with the title *All About Plants* **A**

2. by Roald Dahl **D**

3. about karate _____

4. with the title *The Adventures of Tom Sawyer* _____

5. by Louise Ross _____

6. with the title *A Wrinkle in Time* _____

7. by Ernest Hemingway _____

8. about music _____

9. with the title *Saving Our Planet* _____

10. by Jack London _____

11. about dogs _____

12. with the title *Great Inventors* _____

13. by Aristotle _____

14. with the title *Roll of Thunder, Hear My Cry* _____

15. about biology _____

The Library

What words do you know in the library?

We learned more words in the library. We learned:
dictionary, encyclopedia, biography, fiction and nonfiction.

One of the reference books in the library is
the dictionary. It tells us about words.

sub·ject | sŭb′jĭkt | —*noun, plural* **subjects 1.** Something that is thought about, discussed, or is the object of an action. **2.** A course or area of study. **3.** A person or thing that is used as the object of a special study. **4.** Someone who is under the control of or owes allegiance to a government or ruler. **5.** A word or group of words in a sentence that does or receives the action of the verb. In the sentences *Jimmy threw the ball, Jill and I went to the movies,* and *The cake tastes good,* the subjects are *Jimmy, Jill and I,* and *The cake.*

One of the reference books is the
encyclopedia. It tells us about people,
places and things.

A biography is a book about someone.
This is a book about Pélé.

A fiction book is a storybook. It tells
a story.

Nonfiction books are not stories.
They are true.

Library

Our teacher took the class to the library and said, "I want
you to get a book to read."

Iliana said, "I want a biography."

Chan said, "I like fiction."

I wanted to read a nonfiction book. We walked around the
library and looked for books. We saw reference books, too.
They were the encyclopedia and the dictionary.

What words do you know in the library?

A What kind of book is it?

biography   dictionary   encyclopedia   fiction   nonfiction

1. A book that is true is _____.

2. A book that tells us about words is a _____.

3. A book that tells stories is _____.

4. A book that tells us about people, places and things is an

_____.

5. A book about someone is a _____.

B Go to the library. Find two examples of each kind of book.
   Write the titles of the books you found.

1. dictionary _____

_____

2. biography _____

_____

3. fiction _____

_____

4. nonfiction _____

_____

5. encyclopedia _____

_____

The Dictionary

What is in the dictionary?

The dictionary is a book that tells us about words. It tells us what a word means, its definition.

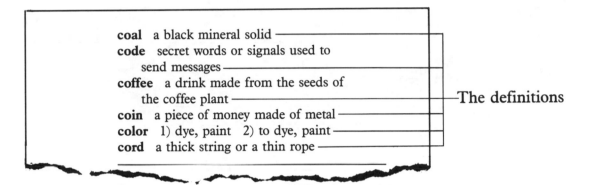

coal   a black mineral solid
code   secret words or signals used to
            send messages
coffee   a drink made from the seeds of
            the coffee plant
coin   a piece of money made of metal
color   1) dye, paint   2) to dye, paint
cord   a thick string or a thin rope

The definitions

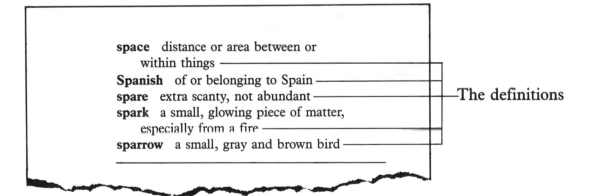

space   distance or area between or
            within things
Spanish   of or belonging to Spain
spare   extra scanty, not abundant
spark   a small, glowing piece of matter,
            especially from a fire
sparrow   a small, gray and brown bird

The definitions

What is in the dictionary?

A Look at the dictionary page and answer the questions.

> **page** 1) one side of a sheet of paper in a book 2) someone who calls people or runs errands
> **pain** the feeling of hurt
> **palm** 1) the inside of your hand between your fingers and your wrist 2) a tall, tropical tree
> **pan** a container with a handle, used for cooking

1. What is one definition of page?

_____

2. Who calls people or runs errands?

_____

3. What is one definition of palm?

_____

4. What kind of feeling is pain?

_____

B Look at the dictionary page and answer the questions.

> **boss** a chief or leader
> **bottle** a container for liquids
> **boulder** a very large rock or stone
> **bowl** a deep, round dish
> **boy** a male child
> **bracelet** a pretty chain or band worn on the arm

1. What is the definition of boss?

_____

2. What is the definition of boulder?

_____

3. What can you find in a bottle?

_____

4. Where do you wear a bracelet?

_____

The Encyclopedia

What is in the encyclopedia?

One of the reference books in the library is the encyclopedia. It gives us information. It tells us about people, places and things. Some encyclopedias have many books or volumes. Like the dictionary, the encyclopedia has the information in alphabetical order.

This encyclopedia has six volumes.

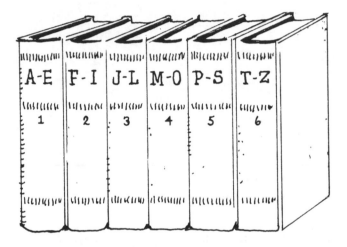

Colombia a country in the northwestern part of South America. The area is 439,920 square miles. The population is 23,331,000. The capital is Bogota.

Columbus, Christopher The discoverer of America (1492). Born in Genoa (1446?), died in Spain (1506). With the help of the Spanish royal family, led an expedition of three ships (Nina, Pinta, Santa Maria) that arrived at land on October 12, 1492.

Coma A kind of deep sleep, usually caused by an accident or illness. The longest coma known is that of Elaine Esposito, who lived in a coma for 37 years, 111 days.

What is in the encyclopedia?

A Where do you look for information on

1. Mexico?   Volume ___4___

2. Jupiter?   Volume _____

3. computers?   Volume _____

4. dinosaurs?   Volume _____

5. eagles?   Volume _____

6. love?   Volume _____

7. biology?   Volume _____

8. soccer?   Volume _____

9. volcanos?   Volume _____

10. Amelia Earhart?   Volume _____

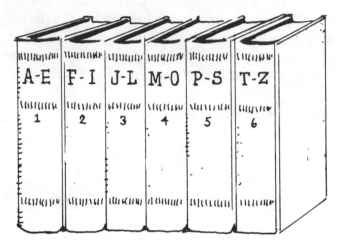

B Where do you look for information?

1. Volume ___1___   I live in Chicago, and I want to learn about it.

2. Volume _____   My Science teacher said to find out about electricity.

3. Volume _____   I want to find out more about the first computers.

4. Volume _____   My Music teacher said to read about the guitar.

5. Volume _____   My Social Studies teacher said to write a paper about China.

6. Volume _____   I am going to California, and I want to find out about it.

7. Volume _____   My Math teacher said to learn all about the meaning of pi.

8. Volume _____   I want to learn more about Martin Luther King.

9. Volume _____   I need to know something about telephones and their history.

10. Volume _____   My English teacher wants a report about languages.

The Table of Contents

What is a Table of Contents, and how do you use it?

You will find a Table of Contents in the front of many books. Often only the word Contents is used. It shows where to find information in the book. It is not in alphabetical order. It gives the information in the order that it comes in the book. The first part of the Table of Contents has the information on the first part of the book. For example, here is part of the Table of Contents for a book on the environment.

CONTENTS

Some fiction books have Tables of Contents, too. Here is an example:

CONTENTS

The Table of Contents: How do you use it?

A Use this Table of Contents to answer the questions.

AMERICAN HISTORY

1. What chapters tell about the United States (or America) before the Revolutionary War? _____

2. On what page does the chapter on the war begin? _____

3. What chapter tells about the United States after the Revolution? _____

4. What chapter tells about the people who lived in America before the Spanish, English and Dutch came here? _____

5. What chapter should you read to learn about life in the American colonies? _____

The Index

What is an index, and how do you use it?

Many books have an index in the back. The index has more
information than the Table of Contents. The index is in
alphabetical order and shows the page where you can find
particular information. Many textbooks have indexes. Here
is part of the index in the back of a history book:

> Immigrants, contributions of, 312–313
> Immigration: and close of frontier, 197; reasons for, 305;
>   history of, 306–308; laws, 308–311, 510; and growth
>   of cities, 345
> Immigration quotas, 309–311
> Impeachment, 61; of Andrew Johnson, 181; and Nixon,
>   448–449.

In this book you will find information on impeachment
on page 61. If you want to read about an impeachment, you
can look on page 181 for the impeachment of Andrew
Johnson.

Here is part of the index in a science book:

> smog, 667, 672
> snail, 141
> snake (see also rattlcsnake)
>   feeding, 170
>   pine, 640

The Index: How do you use it?

A Use the index to find the answers.

1. Where is the information on Science words? _____

2. Where is the information on Computer vocabulary? _____

3. Where is the information on school subjects? _____

4. Where is the information on how to do Math problems? _____

5. Where is the information on Music words? _____

B Use the index to find the answers.

1. On what page can you find out about the pine snake? _____

2. Where do you find information on the snail? _____

3. What pages tell about smog? _____

4. How do you find out about feeding snakes? _____

The Newspaper Index

What do you know about the newspaper?

When I read the newspaper, I use the index. I look in the index to find the <u>news</u>, <u>sports</u>, information on <u>TV-radio</u> and on <u>Help Wanted</u>.

A newspaper tells us the important things that are happening. It tells us the news.

There is a part of the newspaper that tells us about what is happening in sports.

I can find out what is on TV or radio. I look in the index under TV or Television. It lists all the programs.

8:00	2	Home Improvement
	4	Movie— "Airplane"
	5	Amazing Animals
	7	A Different World
	9	Washington Week in Review

A part of the paper has the Help Wanted ads. When I need a job I look at that part of the paper.

SECRETARY male/female good skills
top salary good benefits
Call 555-5123

What do you know about the newspaper?

A   Use the newspaper index to find the answers.

Around the Nation	6
Books	16
Business	31–41
Crossword	16
Editorials	24
Movies	12–16
Sports	19–23
TV/Radio	51
Weather	23

Where would you find

1. information on new books and authors? _____

2. what is on television at 9 tonight? _____

3. today's business news? _____

4. the latest baseball scores? _____

5. tomorrow's weather? _____

6. what's happening in other cities? _____

B   Some newspapers have more than one part. Each part has a letter and page number.

INTERNATIONAL:
Second Coca-Cola factory opens in China	B3
African nations hold meeting	A1
Anti-war conference opens in Berlin	A18

NATIONAL:
Texas is fastest-growing state	A2
Miami opens heart to lost child	A1
Washington senator to marry	B8

Use the index to answer these questions:

1. There are two parts to this newspaper. What are the letters for the two parts? _____

2. What page has information about Texas? _____

3. What is happening in Berlin? _____

4. Who is getting married? _____

5. Where can you find information on China? _____

The Telephone Directory

What do you know about the telephone directory?

When I want to call someone, I use the telephone directory. Words that I need to know are emergency, information, long distance, yellow pages and white pages.

In an emergency you look in the front of the telephone directory. It has the telephone number that you call. In many cities the number is 911.

When you don't know the number to call, look in the front of the phone book for the information number. Look for Directory Assistance.

Illinois Bell ready reference:

Public Offices
See Customer Guide page 2

Directory Assistance
Within Area   **411**
Outside Area   **Area Code + 555-1212**
"800 Service" numbers **800 + 555-1212**

Repair Service 611

You can call another city or another country. This is called long distance.

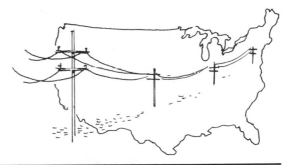

When you want to know the telephone number of a company or a store or a friend, you can look in the white pages, the telephone directory that is in alphabetical order. When you don't know the name of the company or the store you can look in the yellow pages under the kind of company or store.

What do you know about the telephone directory?

A Where do you get the information?

emergency   information   long distance   white pages   yellow pages

1. You look in the _____ for a friend's number.

2. You call _____ when you don't know the number.

3. When you need police officers or fire fighters, you call the _____ number.

4. When you call another city, you are using _____.

5. You look in the _____ under the kind of company or business.

B Where do you get the information?

1. I want to call my friend Sam Spade.   *Look in the white pages.*

2. I want to call a store that sells books.   _____

3. I want to call my school and the number isn't in the telephone directory.   _____

4. My brother lives in another city.   _____

5. There is an automobile accident.   _____

C Use this part of an index for the yellow pages to answer the questions.

Dials	459	Diapers	465
Diamond appraisers	110	Diaries	465
Diamond buyers	459	Dictating machines	465
Diamond cutters	460	Diesel engines	565
Diamond rings	805	Diesel fuel	359

1. On what page are the stores that have diamond rings? _____

2. Where can you find out which stores have diapers? _____

3. You are an executive, and you need a dictating machine. Where do you look? _____

4. Your car takes diesel fuel. Where do you find the places you can buy it? _____

5. You need a diary. Where do you find the stores that sell diaries? _____

Schedules

How do you read schedules?

When you want information, it is important to know how to read different kinds and styles of writing. One different kind of writing is schedules.

Many schedules are easy to read. Radio and television schedules show what is on every half-hour during the day. They look like this:

SUNDAY
8:00
2   Movie
4   Local news
5   Sports special
7   Mystery show
9   Interview show

When you read this schedule you can see what is on each channel at 8 o'clock.

Some schedules are more difficult to read because they use short versions or abbreviations of words you know. On a bus schedule, for example, you must know these abbreviations:

Arr	means	Arrival (when the bus comes)
Dep	means	Departure (when the bus leaves)
L	means	Local (a bus that has several stops)
E	means	Express (a bus that goes directly to one place)
PM	means	after 12 Noon to midnight
AM	means	after midnight to 12 Noon

How do you read schedules?

A Here is part of a bus schedule. Reading the schedule from top to bottom, use it to answer the questions below.

		#5 L	#111 L	#900 E
Madison	Dep	5:00PM	6:00PM	8:00AM
Wikkawikka	Dep	5:14PM	6:14PM	—
Middletown	Dep	5:38PM	6:38PM	—
Red Barn	Dep	—	6:50PM	—
Mt. Morris	Dep	6:15PM	7:20PM	9:20AM

1. What is the number of the only morning bus to Mt. Morris? _____

2. What time does the bus for Red Barn leave from Madison? _____

3. When does the express bus leave Madison? _____

4. It's 6:05 PM, and I'm in Wikkawikka. What is the number of the next bus I can take to Mt. Morris? _____

5. It's 6:10 PM, and I'm in Madison. What is the number of the next bus I can take to Mt. Morris? _____

6. I'm taking the bus from Red Barn. When will I get to Mt. Morris? _____

B Here is part of a television schedule. Use it to answer the questions below.

TV THIS EVENING
6:00
    2 News
    4 News
    5 Star Trek
    9 Candid Camera
6:30
    2 ABC News
    4 CBS News
    9 News, Sports

1. What time is the news on Channel 9? _____

2. When can you watch "Star Trek"? _____

3. How many channels have news at 6:00? _____

4. How many channels have news at 6:30? _____

How do you read schedules?

Sometimes you must read a schedule because you are
meeting someone. Often bus or train stations and airports
have television sets that show only schedule information.
Sometimes this information includes other abbreviations
that you should know. These could be

Fl #	which means	Flight Number (the number of the airplane)
St	which means	Stops (the places where the airplane stops)
ETA	which means	Estimated Time of Arrival (when the airplane will probably arrive)
DST	which means	Daylight Saving Time, a change of time from April to October in some parts of the world
OT	which means	On Time
Gate	which means	the place where the airplane is arriving or from which it leaves.

Many times a schedule may seem difficult to read. It is
important to look at the information below or above the
schedule. This usually explains any abbreviations you do
not know. Pay attention to little marks like this * or this †.
They may be on the schedule. The explanation for them is
above or below the schedule, also.

How do you read schedules?

A There are a number of people at the airport looking at the schedule behind the airline counter. Help them find the information they need.

	Arr	Dep	From	To	Information	Gate
			A-ONE AIRWAYS			
Flt 201	5:15	7:30	Chicago	NYC	OT	4
Flt 202	—	6:00	—	Omaha	OT	5
Flt 210	5:45	—	Denver	—	ETA—6:00	8
Flt 208	6:15	7:00	Omaha	NYC	ETA—6:30	7

1. Ms. Miller is waiting for her husband, who is flying in from Denver. What time will the plane arrive? _____

2. The Wang family is going to Omaha. What is the number of the gate to which they should go? _____

3. Mary Fredericks has a friend arriving from Chicago. What time will his plane arrive? _____

4. What is the number of the flight probably arriving at 6:30? _____

5. Which two flights are late? _____

6. I am going to New York City (NYC). What is the earliest time I can leave? _____

7. Louise is waiting at Gate 7. Where is the plane coming from that will arrive there? _____

B Complete the definitions.

1. Flt   means _____

2. Arr   means _____

3. Dep   means _____

4. OT   means _____

5. ETA   means _____

Diagrams

How do you read diagrams?

Sometimes in a book you will see line drawings that are
called diagrams. These diagrams are pictures of
information. You need to understand them when you read.
You may also want to use a diagram when you are writing a
composition. You need to understand how diagrams give
you information.

There are several kinds of diagrams. An easy one to
understand is a box diagram. This organizational diagram is
an example of a box diagram.

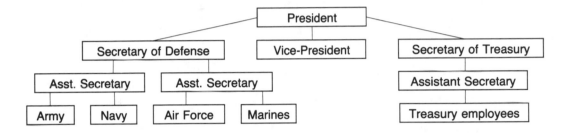

This organizational diagram shows you part of the
organization of a country's government. Basically, it shows
who leads which people, or is their boss.

Here is another kind of diagram. It is called a line chart.
This one shows how much money a company has made in
the first three months of the year:

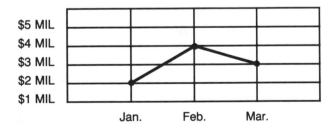

This diagram is a fast way to show that the company sales
were higher in February. It also shows exactly how high the
sales were. Diagrams show information in a way that is
quick to see and understand.

How do you read diagrams?

A Use the organizational chart to answer the questions.

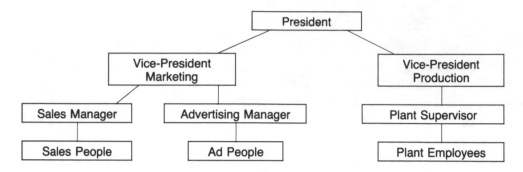

1. Who is the boss of the Advertising Manager? _____

2. Who is under the Vice-President for Production? _____

3. Who is the boss of the sales people? _____

4. Who does each vice-president work for? _____

5. Who is the boss of the plant employees? _____

6. How many vice-presidents are there? _____

B Use the line chart of sales at American Pie to answer
the questions.

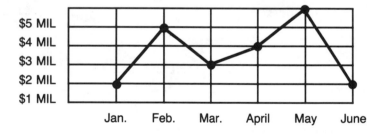

1. During which two months did the company sell $2 million? _____

2. What was the best month for sales? _____

3. What was the next best month for sales? _____

4. In which month did the company sell $3 million? _____

5. Do pies sell better in March or May? _____

6. Are sales better in January or April? _____

Diagrams

How do you read diagrams?

There are two more kinds of diagrams that are used often.
Like the others, they help give information quickly and
easily.

Another kind of diagram is called the bar chart. This is a
diagram which looks like this:

MONTHLY EXPENSES

Rent	$315.00
Food	$300.00
Clothing	$150.00
Transportation	$50.00
Entertainment	$25.

A bar chart is very much like a line chart, but some people
find it easier to read.

A pie chart is easy to read, also. It looks like a pie. The
same information above would look like this in a pie chart:

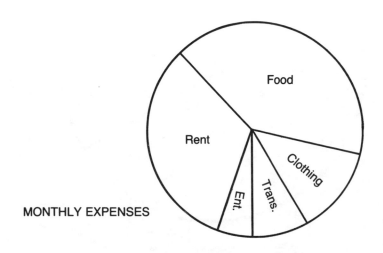

MONTHLY EXPENSES

How do you read diagrams?

A Here is some information and a blank chart. Put the information on the chart.

> The Chang family earns $1200 a month. They spend $400 on rent, $400 on food, $100 on clothing, $150 on transportation and $150 on entertainment.

MONTHLY EXPENSES

B Use the information above to complete the pie chart below.

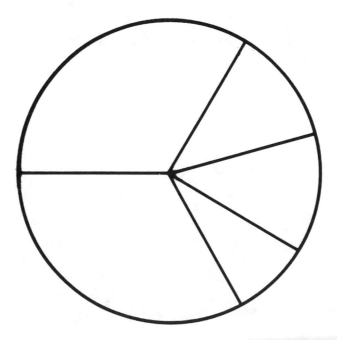

Doing Homework

How can you be a better student?

Homework can help you be a better student. Homework helps you understand what you have learned in class. Homework is an important part of learning in every subject. How can you do homework better?

1. Copy the homework assignment in class and be sure that you understand it. When you don't understand, ask your teacher questions before you leave.

2. Take your books home from school every day.

3. Have a special place at home to do your homework. It helps to have a desk, but a table will do.

4. Do your homework every day. Sometimes it is easy to forget, especially when there is something interesting to watch on television or do with your friends. Your homework is more important.

Do you know how to read homework assignments? Here is what Stephan's teacher wrote:

> pp. 18-25. Ques. 1-5, p. 26. Memorize paragraph 1 p. 18.

This assignment says: Read pages 18-25. Answer questions 1-5 on page 26. Memorize the first paragraph on page 18. pp. means <u>pages</u>. p. means <u>page</u>. Ques. means <u>question</u>.

 RULE: Do your homework all the time because it is important.

How can you be a better student?

A What is your H.Q.? (Homework Quotient). Write the letter of the correct answer on the line to the right:

1. You have homework in Social Studies, but you forgot to copy the assignment down. What do you do?
a) Forget it.   b) Tell your teacher you did the homework but left it at home.   c) Call a friend for the information.   _____

2. You have a report due in Science next week. What do you do now?
a) Watch television because you won't have time next week.   b) Forget it till next week.   c) Get started on the report now.   _____

3. You don't understand part of the Math homework. What do you do?
a) Do what you can and remember to ask questions next time.   b) Don't do anything and tell the teacher you didn't understand.   c) Tell the teacher that your dog ate your homework.   _____

4. You were sick last week and missed two days of school. What do you do?
a) Forget it and hope the teacher will, too.   b) Ask the teacher for the homework you missed and do it.
c) Copy the homework from a friend.   _____

5. Your friend is having a big party tonight, and you have a lot of homework. What do you do?
a) Do the homework before you go to the party.
b) Come home from the party and do the homework.
c) Plan to be sick tomorrow.   _____

Your Homework Quotient: 4-5 correct answers—You're doing a good job.
3 correct answers—You're doing O.K., but try harder.
1-2 correct answers—Change your homework habits now.

Taking Tests

How do you complete answer sheets?

Sometimes when you take a test you must use a special answer sheet. The answer sheet is read by a machine. It is important to complete the answer sheet correctly.

1. Always use a pencil. Make your marks very black for the machine to read them.

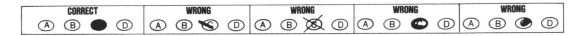

2. Begin writing information from the left to the right. Put one letter in every box. Mark one letter in every column. Put your last name, then your first name.

    EXAMPLE: John Brown = Brown John

    NAME
    LAST   FIRST
    | B | R | O | W | N | | | J | O | H | N | | | |

3. When you write numbers, write one number in every box. Mark one number in every column.

    EXAMPLE: December 6 =   1 2   0 6

4. Use the last 2 numbers of the year you were born.

    EXAMPLE: 1980 = 8 0

    DATE OF BIRTH
    MO. DAY YR
    | 1 | 2 | 0 | 6 | 8 | 0 |

5. Mark one answer for every question. Never mark two answers.

    EXAMPLE: a ( )   b ●   c ●   WRONG
    　　　　　　 a ( )   b ●   c ( )   CORRECT

 **Remember, the machine is not your teacher.**
Check to be sure all information is correct!

How do you complete answer sheets?

A Complete the answer sheets with the information.

EXAMPLE: John Miller of Class 801. Birthday is
September 1, 1976.

NAME				
LAST		FIRST	CLASS	DATE OF BIRTH MO. DAY YR

NAME
LAST   FIRST   CLASS   DATE OF BIRTH MO. DAY YR

| M | I | L | L | E | R | | | J | O | H | N | | | |

| 8 | 0 | 1 |

| 0 | 9 | 0 | 1 | 7 | 6 |

1. Rose Luccio of Class 961. Birthday is May 10, 1979.

NAME
LAST   FIRST   CLASS   DATE OF BIRTH MO. DAY YR

2. James Brand of Class 532. Birthday is November 8, 1980.

NAME
LAST   FIRST   CLASS   DATE OF BIRTH MO. DAY YR

B Mark the answer sheet with the correct answer:

EXAMPLE: He is a

    a) book   b) school   c) student   a ( )   b ( )   c ( )

1. I am learning

    a) English   b) book   c) pencil   a ( )   b ( )   c ( )

2. Science is a

    a) English   b) subject   c) Math   a ( )   b ( )   c ( )

3. We are in

    a) table   b) friend   c) school   a ( )   b ( )   c ( )

4. The sun is a

    a) star   b) flower   c) rain   a ( )   b ( )   c ( )

5. Two plus two is

    a) eight   b) three   c) four   a ( )   b ( )   c ( )

6. In the library there are

    a) books   b) weather   c) country   a ( )   b ( )   c ( )

More about Taking Tests

Do you know how to take a test?

Some tests ask you to put two parts of an answer together.
Usually one part of the answer is on the left side of the
paper, and the other part of the answer is on the right side
of the paper. This kind of test may look like this:

DIRECTIONS: Read Column A, then look at Column B
for the answer. Put the numbers of the correct answers on
the lines beside Column B.

WHERE DO YOU FIND IT?

Column A	Column B	
1. the sports news	1. in the library	_____3_____
2. an encyclopedia	2. in a Social Studies book	_____1_____
3. a map	3. in a newspaper	_____2_____

Sometimes the instructions are like this:

INSTRUCTIONS: Draw a line from the answer
in Column A that matches (goes with) the answer in
Column B:

Column A | Column B
1. an addition problem — 1. in Science class
2. a book on plants — 2. in English class
3. a dictionary — 3 in Math class

Sometimes you use letters:

DIRECTIONS: Put the letter of the correct answer on
the line beside each place:

_____b_____	1. my classroom	a. at home
_____c_____	2. my food	b. in school
_____a_____	3. my family	c. in the supermarket

Do you know how to take a test?

A Follow the directions.

1. INSTRUCTIONS: Put the letter of the correct answer on the line beside each place:

_____ 1. We paint pictures   **a.** in Computer.

_____ 2. We work with programs   **b.** in Music.

_____ 3. We sing songs   **c.** in Art.

2. INSTRUCTIONS: Draw a line from the answer in Column A that matches (goes with) the answer in Column B.

Column A	Column B
1. the emergency number	**1.** in the classroom
2. a fiction book	**2.** in the library
3. a notebook	**3.** in the telephone directory

B Write the missing instructions.

DIRECTIONS: _____

_____

Column A	Column B	
1. the back of a book	**1.** the television schedule	_3_
2. a dictionary	**2.** what a word means	_2_
3. a newspaper	**3.** an Index	_1_

C Complete the sentences.

Put the letter of the correct answer on the line beside each place.

_____ 1. You draw lines   **a.** on the line beside each place.

_____ 2. You write a word   **b.** to match columns.

_____ 3. You put the letter of the correct answer   **c.** when a word is missing in a sentence.

More about Taking Tests

Do you know how to take a test?

Some tests have sentences with a missing word or words.
Sometimes the missing words are listed, and you must write
them in. That kind of test looks like this:

DIRECTIONS: Write in the missing words:

good   he   students   teacher

I like my Social Studies _____*teacher*_____. __*He*__ is very nice.
                              1   2

He likes to help his _____*students*_____. He is a _____*good*_____ teacher.
                          3   4

Sometimes there are many words listed, and you must
decide which ones to use. That kind of test looks like this:

DIRECTIONS: Select the correct missing word and write
it on the line:

1. "Did you _____*read*_____ the book?" asked the teacher.
   watch   read   sing

2. My father is a tall _____*man*_____.
   woman   boy   man

Sometimes there are no words listed. Then you must
think of the missing word or words and write it in. That
kind of test looks like this:

DIRECTIONS: Write in the missing word.

1. The country that I live in now is called _*the United States*_.

2. A city has many streets, buildings, and _____*people*_____.

Do you know how to take a test?

A Follow the instructions.

1. INSTRUCTIONS: Write in the missing words:
        friends   homework   morning   school   talk

Every ____*morning*____ I walk to _____. I meet my _____,
               1   2   3

and we _____ about the _____.
                4   5

2. DIRECTIONS: Select the correct missing word and write it on the line:

   1. Shana was painting a _____.
       television   picture   book

   2. "What did you _____ on television?" my father asked me.
       read   sing   watch

B Write the missing directions.

1. DIRECTIONS: _____

_____

   1. In Social Studies we are studying ____*American*____ history.

   2. There are fifty ____*states*____ in the United States.

2. INSTRUCTIONS: _____

_____

      do   emergency   help   police officer

My brother is a ____*police officer*____. He likes to ____*help*____ people.
                       1   2

He is very good in an ____*emergency*____. He always knows what to ____*do*____.
                             3   4

Studying for Tests

How do you study for tests?

Every student takes tests. Tests help you and the teacher know what you have learned. It is important to know how to take tests. It is important, too, to know what to study for your tests.

Teachers usually tell students what to study for a test. They use the word "review." What is a review?

Review means to go over something again. When you review you go over the information you have learned. Here is an example.

Ran Shu's English teacher said, "On Friday we will have a test on all the vocabulary words we have studied since September. Be sure to review them all."

That night Ran Shu went home and took out all his vocabulary papers. He took out his weekly vocabulary tests, too. First he read the words again. Then he looked at his tests. He looked especially at the words he didn't know on the weekly tests. Then he made a list of those words. He read the lists many times.

The next day Ran Shu went home with his friend Ben. He took his papers. He and Ben asked each other the vocabulary words. First he would give Ben a meaning and then Ben would say the word. Then Ben would ask him a meaning, and he would say the word.

The next morning he and Ben smiled at each other before English class. They knew the vocabulary words for the test and would probably each get a good grade.

 **RULE:** **When you review you go over the information several times. It helps to review with a friend.**

How do you study for tests?

A Write the letter of the correct action on the line to
the right.

1. Your Science teacher says, "Tomorrow we will have a
test on the Astronomy unit." What do you do?
a) Review the unit in the book.   b) Review the papers
the teacher gave you on Astronomy.   c) Do both a)
and b).   _____

2. Your Math teacher says, "The class will have a test
tomorrow on the multiplication of fractions." What
do you do?
a) Review your Math papers to see what mistakes you
made in the problems and why.   b) Review the
chapter in your Math book on multiplication of
fractions.   c) Do both a) and b).   _____

3. Your Social Studies teacher says, "On Monday we will
have a test on the unit we have been studying." What
do you do?
a) Review everything you have had this year.
b) Review the unit your class has just finished.
c) Do both a) and b).   _____

B What would you review? Write the answer after every
question.

1. Your Social Studies teacher says, "On Monday we are
going to have a test on the three parts of the United
States government."

_____

2. Your Math teacher says, "This afternoon we will have a
test after lunch on the addition of decimals."

_____

3. Your Science teacher says, "Tomorrow you will take a
test on Chapters One through Four in your book."

_____

Memorizing

How do you memorize information?

When you study for a test, sometimes it helps to memorize the information. Here is a way you can memorize lists.

1. Take a piece of notebook paper and fold it in half the long way. Open it and write on it the information you want to memorize. Put part of the information on the left side and part of the information on the right side.

2. Read the information. Then close your eyes and say that information. Open your eyes and see if you remembered everything. Do this again. Keep doing it until you are sure that you know all the information.

3. Fold the paper again. Look at only one side of the paper. Say the information on the other side, the side you can't see. Were you right? Check and see. Then fold the paper and look at the other side of the paper. Try to remember what is written on the side you can't see. Soon you will know everything on both sides of the paper.

 **RULE:** **You can get better grades on tests when you memorize information.**

How do you memorize information?

A How would you memorize this information?

1. Vocabulary words and their meanings.

   On the left side of the paper, I would write _____

   On the right side of the paper, I would write _____

2. The three branches of government and what each does.

   On the left side of the paper, I would write _____

   On the right side of the paper, I would write _____

3. The parts of the digestive system and what each does.

   On the left side of the paper, I would write _____

   On the right side of the paper, I would write _____

B Here is a problem in memorizing. Turn to page 10.
Copy the dictionary page with the words <u>page</u>, <u>pain</u>,
<u>palm</u>, and <u>pan</u> on a paper. Copy the words on the
left side and the definitions on the right side.
Memorize the words and definitions. Now answer
these questions:

1. What is one definition of <u>palm</u>?

   _____

2. What is a container used for cooking?

   _____

3. What is one definition of <u>page</u>?

   _____

4. What is the word for "a tall tropical tree"?

   _____

Writing Reports—Composition Form

How do you do reports for your teachers?

Your teachers will ask you to write reports for different classes. Your English teacher will ask you to write a book report. Your Social Studies and your Science teachers will ask you to write reports, also. It is important to understand what to do when you write a report.

A report or a composition usually has a particular form. This is the pattern of a short report:

TEACHER'S NAME	YOUR NAME
CLASS NAME	DATE

TITLE OF REPORT

1) _____

2) _____

3) _____

_____

_____

It is important to remember that you indent the first word of each paragraph. To indent means to begin about 1 inch to the right of the margin, as on line 1 above. The other lines begin at the margin, as in lines 2 and 3.

When you are writing a long report, you should put the first information on a page by itself. It is called a title page and looks like this:

Mr. Johnson   Emily Rodriguez
Science   October 18, 1993

Different Families of Plants

How do you do reports?

A Here is some information. Copy it in the correct form for a report:

John Thomas is writing a report for Social Studies. The report is on "The Industrial Revolution." His teacher's name is Ms. Selden. Today's date is March 6, 1993.

_____   _____

_____   _____

_____

B Here is some information. Copy it in the correct form for a report:

Susana Campo is writing a book report for her English teacher, Mr. Jones. She is writing the report on a book she read. The title of the book is _Life on the Mississippi_, written by Mark Twain. Write today's date.

_____   _____

_____   _____

_____

C Here is the first paragraph of John Thomas' report on the Industrial Revolution. Copy it in the correct form for his report.

The Industrial Revolution was an exciting time in the United States. It was a revolution without guns. It made as big a difference in life, though, as a war with armies.

_____

_____

_____

Book Reports

How do you do write a book report?

When you read a book for English, your teacher will ask
you to write a report. How do you do it?

1. Write the name of the book and the name of the author.
   Most teachers want you to do this as the title of your
   paper. It should look like this:

   The Adventures of Juan Bobo
   by
   Mary Johnstone

2. Write something about the book. You can write about the story or
   about something that happened in the story. This is an example:

   > This is a book about the funny things that happened to
   > Juan Bobo. In the beginning everyone thought Juan was
   > stupid. In the end he always did all right for himself.
   >
   > or
   >
   > Juan Bobo has many funny adventures in this book. One
   > of them happened when he was selling his cow. Everyone
   > tried to get his cow without paying him money. In the end
   > he had more money and still had his cow, too.

3. Say whether you liked or didn't like the book, and tell
   why. This is an example:

   > I liked this book very much. I think everyone can learn
   > something from Juan Bobo.
   >
   > or
   >
   > I didn't like this book. I don't think it was nice to make
   > fun of someone like Juan Bobo.

How do you write a book report?

A Here is a book report. What is missing?

The title _____

The author _____

The story _____

Like/Didn't like _____

An Interesting Life
by
John Sargent

    I didn't like this book because it wasn't interesting. I don't think Mr. Sargent had an interesting life.

B Write a book report on a book you have read. Use this form.

_____

_____

_____

_____

_____

_____

_____

_____

_____

_____

Information Reports

How do you write an information report?

Sometimes your teachers will ask you to write an information report. You can get the information from reference books and other books in the library. How do you do it?

1. Decide the subject of your report, what it will be about. The subject of a report can be a country, a person, a thing or how something is done. Here are some examples:

    > Janine must write a report for Social Studies. Her class is studying Latin America. She will write a report on Panama.

    > Noel's class is learning about American history. He must write a report. His subject will be George Washington.

    > Bob's Science teacher asked him to write a report for Astronomy. He wants to write about America's space program.

2. Go to the library and look in the card catalog under your subject. Copy the names and the numbers of the books on your subject from the cards. Find the books or ask the librarian where to find them. If you have a library card, take the books home and read them.

3. Go to the library reference books. There may be more than one encyclopedia there. Look in all of them for information on your subject. You can't take the encyclopedia home with you. You must use it in the library.

 **RULE** **Find at least two books with information on your subject.**

How do you write an information report?

A Put the letter of the subject on the line next to each report title.

    a. Science   **1.** "My Country"   _____

    b. Social Studies   **2.** "A Talking Machine"   _____

    c. Music   **3.** "History of the City Museum"   _____

    d. Art   **4.** "The First Man on the Moon"   _____

    e. Computers   **5.** "The History of the Piano"   _____

                           6. "The Human Body"   _____

B Your Science class is studying animals. Everyone must write a report. You like cats, so you are going to write a report on "Cats."

Go to the library and look in the card catalog under "Cats." What are some of the books on cats? Copy the author and title of at least two books here:

_____

_____

C In Social Studies you are studying World War II. You must write a report about an important part of the war. You decide to write about "D-Day."

Go to the library and look in the card catalog. Look up the headings "D-Day" and "World War II, Invasion of Europe." Copy the author and title of at least two books you find listed:

_____

_____

More on Information Reports

How do you write an information report?

When you find information for your report, use it. That
means you must copy the information. How do you do it?

1. Write down the title of the book, the author,
   the publishing company and the date of the book. Do it
   like this:

> Crime and Punishment, Fyodor Dostoevsky, The Modern
> Library, 1978

> A Wrinkle in Time, Madeleine L'Engle,
> Ariel Books, 1962

2. Write down the page number where the information is.
   When you use the information in your report, you will
   want to say exactly where you found it in the book.

3. When you copy the exact words in the book, put the
   quotation marks (") before and after the words like this:

> p. 41 "George Washington was a popular leader. His tired
> and hungry volunteers did not blame him for their
> troubles."

4. Make a list of all the books that you used for your
   report. This list is called a bibliography. Put it on a
   piece of paper at the end of your report, like this:

BIBLIOGRAPHY

Panama Canal, Orlando Martinez, Gordon and Cremonesi, 1978
A Trip Through Panama, Nancy Ames, Tobo Publications, 1975
The History of Panama, Tom Ford, Voluntad Publishers, 1989
The Encyclopedia Britannica, Volume 8, 1990

How do you write an information report?

A Go to the library and find two books about football or your favorite sport. Write down the information you need on the title, author, publishing company and date.

1. _____

_____

2. _____

_____

3. _____

_____

B Open the books to page 10 or 11. Copy two sentences from the first book here:

1. (p. ___) "_____

_____

_____"

Copy two sentences from the second book here:

2. (p. ___) "_____

_____

_____"

C Write a bibliography for a report on football or your favorite sport here:

BIBLIOGRAPHY

_____

_____

_____

_____

The Outline

How do you write an information report?

When you have all the information you need for your
report, you must write it. How do you do that?

1. Decide how you are going to give the information. Make
   an outline.
   An outline is a plan of what you will say in the
   beginning of the report, in the middle and at the end.
   This is an outline:

   ### GEORGE WASHINGTON

   1. His early years
   2. His life as a soldier in the Indian Wars
   3. His life as a planter
   4. The Commander-in-Chief of the American Army
   5. The first President

2. Organize the information you have. Sometimes it helps
   to write the book and page numbers of information
   under the part of the outline where you will use it. Your
   outline might be like this:

   1. His early years
      The Young George Washington, page 8
      The Cherry Tree, page 4

3. Write your report. Read it through and correct
   everything. When you are sure it is good, copy it. Have
   a separate page for the cover with your name and the
   title of your report. Have a separate page for the
   bibliography, too.

 **RULE: Always correct your report and copy it again.**

How do you write an information report?

A Abdul's Social Studies teacher asked him to write a report on his country. He went to the library and found some information. He has information on the history of his country, the geography, the way people live there, and the politics. Write Abdul's outline for him:

MY COUNTRY

1. _____

2. _____

3. _____

4. _____

B The Science teacher asked Chim to write a report on goldfish. She went to the library and found out where goldfish come from, how to take care of goldfish, and a story about a goldfish who rang a bell for its dinner. Write Chim's outline for her:

GOLDFISH

1. _____

2. _____

3. _____

C Louise's English teacher asked her to write a report on her favorite author. Louise went to the library to find the information. She found out how many books her author wrote and what their titles are. She found out the names of the prizes some of the author's books won. She found out where the author was born and where he lives. Write Louise's outline for her:

MY FAVORITE AUTHOR

1. _____ **3.** _____

2. _____ **4.** _____

The Summary

What is a summary?

When you use information in a report, sometimes you copy the words that are written in a book. Sometimes you don't want to use every word. Then you write a summary.

A summary is something short. It gives only the important information. Here are some examples:

"It was an exciting game. In the first half the Blues made two touchdowns and scored one field goal. In the second half, however, the Golds made a comeback. 'Brains' Bikowski, their quarterback, led them to three winning plays, and the Golden boys won again with a final 19 to 17.

SUMMARY: In the Gold-Blue game the Golds won 19-17.

"Wheat is one of the most common cereals. It is grown all over the world, especially in North America, Europe and Asia. It is less common in Africa, although it was grown there in Egypt many thousands of years ago. It was also grown in China in ancient times, but now rice is the most popular grain there."

SUMMARY: Wheat is a popular cereal most important in North America, Europe and Asia.

What is a summary?

A Choose the best summary for the following paragraph:

"The hummingbird is the smallest of all birds, and there are many different species. These pretty creatures move their wings so quickly that sometimes you cannot see their motion. This helps hummingbirds to hover or stay in one place for some time. They do this to gather the nectar from flowers with their long beaks. Some varieties eat insects, too."

SUMMARY A: Hummingbirds are small birds.
SUMMARY B: Hummingbirds live on nectar and insects.
SUMMARY C: Hummingbirds are small, fast birds that
               live mostly on nectar.   BEST SUMMARY: ＿＿＿

B Write a summary of one or two sentences for this paragraph:

"The life of the early pioneers on America's great plains was not an easy one. Many of them lived in sod houses, partly underground to protect them from the extreme heat of summer and the cold of winter. Terrible storms sometimes destroyed all their food. There were still hostile Indians and dangerous animals. It was lonely, too, in an area where the nearest neighbor could be miles away."

SUMMARY: ＿＿＿＿＿＿＿＿＿＿＿＿＿＿＿＿＿＿＿

＿＿＿＿＿＿＿＿＿＿＿＿＿＿＿＿＿＿＿＿＿＿＿＿＿＿

C You can make summaries of sentences, also. Find the short sentence in Column B that matches the long sentence in Column A. Write its number on the line.

Column A
1. The Asian elephant, with small ears, and the larger African elephant, with big floppy ears, are the only two kinds of elephants on earth.
2. Jupiter is the biggest of all the planets of the solar system—more than eleven times bigger than earth.
3. The highest place in the world is the top of Mount Everest, which stands between the countries of Tibet and Nepal, in Asia.

Column B
A. Jupiter is the biggest planet. ＿＿＿＿
B. There are two kinds of elephants. ＿＿＿＿
C. The top of Mount Everest is the highest place in the world. ＿＿＿＿

How do you understand quickly what you are reading?

You need to read many things for school. It is important to
read quickly. You can learn to read quickly. One way is to
look for the important words in what you are reading.
Here is a sentence:

> The boy in the red coat was walking with his friends.

Here are the important words in the sentence:

> boy   red coat   walking with   friends.

Here is another sentence:

> Many people in my family, including my brothers and sisters,
> are not living in the United States now.

Here are the important words in the sentence:

> Many people   my family   brothers   sisters
> not living   United States now.

The important words in a sentence give you the
information you need to answer the questions: Who or
What? Where? When? How? Why? Look at this sentence:

> When you first learn to ride a bicycle alone, you will find
> that it is difficult to keep balanced without help.

The important words:

> first (when)   ride bicycle (what)   alone (where)
> find difficult (how)   keep balanced without help (why)

How do you understand quickly what you are reading?

A Draw a line under the important words in these
sentences. Check the number of important words on
the line beside the sentence.

1. "You must help me clean the house," said my
   mother. (6)
2. Daniel Boone is one of the best known early American
   frontiersmen. (7)
3. Ranko stayed up late last night, watching an old movie
   on television about some gangsters. (8)
4. When we were walking to school yesterday, we saw an
   automobile accident on our street. (8)
5. Alice and Jean are good friends. (4)

B Use the important words in the sentences below to find
the answers to the questions:

1. My class stayed after three today in
   Ms. Benson's room because we were
   noisy during Science.

WHAT/WHO? _____

WHERE? _____

WHEN? _____

HOW? _____

WHY? _____

2. The window of a second-floor apartment
   in our building was broken yesterday by
   the terrible wind.

WHAT/WHO? _____

WHERE? _____

WHEN? _____

HOW? _____

WHY? _____

3. Jack ordered three hamburgers in the
   fast food place because he was very
   hungry after school.

WHAT/WHO? _____

WHERE? _____

WHEN? _____

HOW? _____

WHY? _____

4. During the second half of the game
   today, the manager sent for a doctor to
   see the injured player.

WHAT/WHO _____

WHERE? _____

WHEN? _____

HOW? _____

WHY? _____

Reading Quickly for Information

How do you understand quickly what you are reading?

One way to read more quickly is to find the important words. Another way to read quickly is to read several words at one time. Many people read like this:

The   tall   man   was   wearing   a   brown   sweater.

It is quicker to read like this:

The tall man   was wearing   a brown sweater.

Your eyes can see more than one word at a time. Your mind can understand a group of words better than one word at a time. You can teach yourself to read several words together.

Try this. When you read the sentences below, look at the dot. Then read the words that are together above the dot. You will be reading more quickly.

"Did you see   where I put   my purse?"   asked Ms. Lane.

The state of California   is very long   and has   a large population.

Yesterday   my friend Ana   invited me   to her house   for dinner.

The art museum   was full   of paintings   and sculptures.

Nancy   was reading   a letter   from her cousin.

 RULE: When you read, read groups of words together.

How do you understand quickly what you are reading?

A Here are sentences with groups of words. Put a dot under each group. Then look at each dot to read the words together.

1. I have   five brothers   living in Texas.

2. The thirteen colonies   wanted independence   and fought   for it.

3. Take the bus   to Jay Street   and walk   six blocks west.

4. Mr. Lee said,   "I had   a hard day   at the office."

5. Susie and Robert   went dancing   after dinner   at a club.

6. "Where   did you go   after school   today?"   she asked.

B These sentences do not have separate groups of words. Put a line after every word group. Then read the sentences by reading the word groups together.

    EXAMPLE: She is / my best friend / in school.

1. Our teacher took the class to the library to find some books.

2. The supermarket was crowded with people buying food for the weekend.

3. "Thank you for the birthday present," said Mrs. Gates to her son.

4. The Sunday newspaper was full of stories about the election.

5. The man at the employment office said that there weren't any jobs.

6. The rock group was giving a concert in the park.

7. The passengers listened to the pilot and the stewardess.

8. Mr. Hyman said, "You watch television too much, young man."

9. Many people believe that world government is possible in the near future.

10. They ate roast beef, rice, vegetables, and apple pie for dinner.

What Information Is Important?

How can you decide what is important?

Many times when you are studying, you must read a lot. Not everything that you read is important. How can you decide? Here is one way: Know the information you need.

Sometimes you must answer questions on what you are reading. Always read the questions first. Here is an example:

Ernesto must read this paragraph and answer these questions:

The fire started at 3 A.M., and the fire fighters came ten minutes later. Sleepy people ran quickly from the building. One woman carried a bird in a cage. By 5 o'clock the apartments were in ruins.

1. When did the fire start?
   a) early in the morning   b) at five o'clock   c) ten minutes later
2. What pet did a woman save?
   a) a bird   b) a cat   c) a dog
3. What kind of building was it?
   a) an office building   b) an apartment building   c) a school

Ernesto read the questions first. Then he looked for the answers. He found the answer to Number 1 in the first sentence. He found the answer to Number 2 in the third sentence. He found the answer to Number 3 in the last sentence. The important sentences in the paragraph were the first, third and fourth.

How can you decide what is important?

A Read the questions, then read the paragraph. Answer the questions after the paragraph.

 1. Who is Olga's best friend?
 2. Where are they going?
 3. Who bought Olga's sweater?

Olga met her best friend Amy on the way to school. They began walking together. "That's a pretty sweater," said Amy. "Is it new?" Olga answered, "Yes, my mother bought it for me yesterday at Tim's Department Store."

1. You can find the answer to the first question in the

   a) last sentence.   b) first sentence.   c) second sentence.   _____

2. You can find the answer to the second question in the

   a) first sentence.   b) second sentence.   c) last sentence.   _____

3. You can find the answer to the third question in the

   a) second sentence.   b) last sentence.   c) first sentence.   _____

4. The important sentences in this paragraph are the

   a) first and last.   b) first and second.   c) second and third.   _____

B Read the questions, then read the paragraph. Draw a line through the sentences that are not important in the paragraph.

 1. Where were Blanche and Henri?
 2. Did Blanche like what she was doing?

Blanche and Henri went to a nice restaurant for dinner. It was expensive, but the food was good. "You look lovely tonight," said Henri. "Thank you," said Blanche, "I'm enjoying myself."

What Information Is Important?

How can you decide what is important?

When you write an information report, it always helps to make an outline. When you read information, an outline can help you decide what information is important and what is not important.

Some authors have an outline in the book. The outline can be the Table of Contents. Sometimes it is part of what you read.

In a Table of Contents the outline can look like this:

AMERICAN HISTORY

Unit One: The First Americans: The first people in America. Where they came from. Where they lived. How they lived.

When the outline is part of what you read, you can understand it by copying the titles of paragraphs or the parts of the paragraphs that look different.

Here is an outline from the titles of paragraphs in a Science book:

The characteristics of bacteria
Growing bacteria
Microscopic study of bacteria
Helpful bacteria
Harmful bacteria

Here is a paragraph that begins with a date. Sometimes the outline in a history book is with dates, in the order of what happened:

1753 Governor Dinwiddie and George Washington

Governor Dinwiddie of Virginia sent George Washington, a twenty-one-year-old major in the Virginia militia, to tell the French to get out of the Allegheny-Monongahela Rivers area. He delivered the message and returned to Richmond.

How can you decide what is important?

A Make an outline of the information on "Taking Tests," "More about Taking Tests" and "Studying for Tests" on pages 31, 33, 35 and 37 in this book. Here is the beginning of the outline to help you.

Page 31   1. Some tests use a special answer sheet.

2. The answer sheet is read by a machine.

Page 33   3. _____

_____

Page 35   4. _____

_____

Page 37   5. _____

_____

B Look at the second chapter in your Social Studies or your Science textbook. Is the important information in the second chapter written differently from other books? Make an outline of the second chapter here:

_____

_____

_____

_____

_____

_____

_____

_____